# FIGHTING THE GOOD FIGHT ON HUNGER AND HOMELESSNESS

# FIGHTING THE GOOD FIGHT ON HUNGER AND HOMELESSNESS

Life Stories And Meeting Inspiring People

## PAUL VENTI

ISBN 978-0-578-859224

Library of Congress Control Number 1-10162480571

Cover Design and Typesetting by Lucy Holtsnider
LucyHoltsnider.com

Edited by Joanne Biondolillo

Printed in the United States of America

Facebook.com/Fighting-The-Good-Fight-On-Hunger-and-Homelessness-1098083563702320

*This book is dedicated to my Mom and Dad who showed me at a young age the meaning of giving and helping others less fortunate. And to all my homeless friends who taught me a life lesson.*

*Acknowledgements. A special thank you to Joanna Biondolillo Author of when I was a child. Steve Zinn Portable showers Barbara Riddleberger Author of heart to heart for the U.A. Journal.Captain Michael Howley South District fire department Middletown Connecticut Dan Drew former mayor of Middletown Connecticut. CTCOSH CT, AFLCIO. All the local unions and folks that have donated to make my mission possible.Joan Campbell for her moral support and making all the food bags and sandwiches.*

# Table of Contents

# 1. Growing Up

I grew up in an Italian household in the small, friendly community of Elmwood, West Hartford, Connecticut. It was a wonderful place for a kid growing up: riding bikes, playing hookie, playing football, basketball, and baseball, and jumping the fence to go swimming after hours at Beachland Park. But it was especially fine to be raised by Italian parents and grandparents that cherished our Italian culture, and celebrated the dreams that being in America allowed you to dream.

Sundays were always a big deal in our two-family home. My siblings and I would wake to the smell of homemade bread baking in the oven and a pot of spaghetti sauce simmering on the stove. Of course, if you didn't eat the bread the same day it was baked, the only thing you could do with it on Monday was use it as a baseball bat, no preservatives! My mom loved to cook and she was very good at it. She also loved to see people enjoy her delicious meals. Every Sunday, the whole family, my brothers, sisters, grandparents and sometimes my aunts, uncles and cousins would sit down to a Sunday feast.

Our meal would start off with warm bread, homemade pasta, meatballs, sausage and braciole. This was followed by a pork roast, turkey or ham. My mom was always the last one to sit down to make sure that everyone's plate was full. We sat for hours eating, talking, laughing.

The food was always plentiful. My folks always instilled in me and my siblings the importance of eating well and feeding others. Having lived through the Great Depression, they knew first hand what it was like to be hungry and to go to bed without having eaten waking only the next morning to wonder again when they might have food.

My mother and my father were placed in an orphanage because my grandparents could simply not afford to feed or cloth them. My dad never talked about it but my mom used to tell me stories of how she and her sisters would eat off of the same plate sharing the small amount of food that they did get at the orphanage. She and her sisters would walk the railroad tracks in Southington trying to find coal that fell of coal cars so that they could heat their home. Whenever my friends walked through the kitchen door; my mom always wanted to feed them. It was simply her way that became our way of growing up and it was a good way.

# 2. Paying it Forward

On February 7, 2010, at 11:17 am, there was a massive explosion at the Klean Energy Power Plant in Middletown, Connecticut.

The explosion took the lives of six Tradesmen and wounded many others. Among them were three good friends of mine from local 777 Connecticut and one Ronnie Crabb being one of my best friends. Old school stand up brothers. I remember that morning well. It was Superbowl Sunday. It was a cold, bitter winter day. But the good people of Middletown came together and in support of our fallen brothers, raised funds for the families who would now be forced to say goodbye to their loved ones.

The First and last Tavern on Main donated fifty pounds of pasta and gallons and gallons of tomato sauce. O'Rourke's Diner donated garlic butter rolls and salad dressings. Local gyms donated fee memberships. Yankee Harley donated a Fatboy Harley to be raffled off. The pasta dinner and fundraiser, held at the newly-built Middletown High School was a big success. We hit it out of the ballpark!

Following that first event, the Lion's Den Boxing Gym hosted an event featuring Jose Canseco rookie of the year and M.V.P for the White Sox. Local businessmen jumped in the ring with him to continue to raise money for the families of the fallen. Even the Middletown police officers, firemen and Union Tradesmen duked it out for the worthy cause.

Inspired by their generosity, I decided to give back to the people of Middletown. I wanted to thank them by organizing two massive food drives. I decided to utilize the mobility I had working as the steward on the clean-up and rebuild of Kleen Energy, which at the time was the largest job in New England. But we were able to fill five pick-up trucks with non-perishable foods that were then donated to the St. Vincent de Paul food pantry and homeless shelter in Middletown.

Not long afterward, I retired and was asked to chair the retirees meeting the local 777. With that, we began Thanksgiving and Christmas food drives and were able to donate literally thousands of pounds of food and gift cards to the AFL-CIO in Rocky Hill, Connecticut. The programs continued to grow and donations from businesses and organizations such as Missions of Mercy and the Connecticut Alliance of Retired Americans helped us to extend our reach to those in need.

# 3. Feeding the Homeless

One afternoon while gassing up my car in Crystal River, Florida, I noticed a group of people giving food to the homeless that were milling about in the gas station parking lot. I approached one of the members in the group and asked how I might volunteer. I was given the contact information for the president of the group known as PHP, People Helping People making arrangements to meet at their food pantry which was really just a rented garage. We spent time sorting nonperishable food. When I was asked if I wanted to go on a food run, I jumped at the opportunity.

Every Thursday and Friday we drove to places known for having those in need and distributed food to as many as we could find. On Sundays, we served dinner at the community center. Eventually, I would meet the homeless at a designated time and location, usually a Walmart or Publix supermarket parking lot. From there, we started to visit homeless camps, the trunk of my car loaded with meals, and blankets donated from local restaurants and nursing homes. Two other volunteers used pickup trucks to deliver meals. Those runs often fed as many as eighty people.

Eventually, the People Helping People President asked me if I would like to be on their board of directors. A brief meeting with the entire board consisted of something like a job interview, after which, I was officially voted in as a member of the board. But that was short lived. I began to realize that I didn't need to drive to the next city or county to fight hunger. Hunger was in my own back yard. I decided to use the money I was spending on gas traveling over to the next county several times a week to buy food and feed the homeless just down the road from my home in Beacon Woods.

# 4. On My Own

Initially, my concerns were to keep the homeless hydrated from continual exposure to the hot Florida sun. I handed out water and snack bars. But it didn't take long to realize that the needs of the homeless far exceeded water and snack bars. I started to buy canned goods, ravioli, puddings, bananas, oranges. The list became longer as they needed so many essentials, toothbrushes, toothpaste, soap, toilet paper. The list was long. With every food and supply run, I was finding more and more people who were homeless. The homeless I encountered always so grateful told me where to find others living in tents and homeless camps. My out of pocket costs were sky rocketing. I was spending anywhere from $800.00 to $1000.00 a month which was coming out of my savings. But it somehow didn't seem that important. The people who depended on me was important so I kept pushing forward, determined not to let any Vet, child or senior to go hungry.

# 5. Fighting the Good Fight

With my savings quickly depleting, I made the decision to sell my United Association pin collection, truly my prized possession. I had been collecting those pins for two and a half decades. Every pin had a history behind it. I had met some amazing brothers and sisters associated with those pins. But I could now see a new purpose for them. The pin site on Facebook that I trade on frowns upon selling them so, in good faith, I assured them that it was not for profit in order to get their blessing. They did give me their blessing. A Union brother from Washington State suggested that I design a pin of my own for Fighting the Good Fight on Hunger and Homelessness. He purchased my new pins in 2018 and 2019 as a donation. I began to use the internet to promote awareness of the hungry and homeless and pin sales increased.

Now with a stream of revenue coming in, I was able to purchase so many needed items, sleeping bags, tents, hoodies, and sneakers. I could get hotel rooms for veterans or those in need of a break from life on the streets. A hot shower, a night in a bed, the simple act of watching a ball game on television where like giving these folks a golden ticket. I was actually making progress.

# 6. 501C-3 NonProfit

As the donations came in, I was able to reach more folks in need. A good friend, who happened to be the business manager of my own local 777, called me one afternoon with a suggestion that would help me take the next steps to solidify my efforts and help even more folks in need. He suggested that I create a 501C3. A nonprofit organization would allow me to take in even more donations and allow those donating to write the donations off on their taxes. This opened the door to donations things like golf charity events. So, I sat down with an attorney and a CPA and got started. There were the usual forms to fill out and filings that were required followed by the usual wait time. But Fighting the Good Fight on Hunger and Homelessness was finally approved as a 501C3, a non-profit! Various members from the local unions were requesting that donations be made to my corporation. Once again, I was able to furnish the food and supplies needed by the homeless.

By this time, I was able to add a Friday night pizza run in addition to several breakfast runs and late afternoon food runs each week. The Dollar Store quickly learned that they would have to restock their shelves after I made a purchase, filling my cart to the brim with the needed food and supplies. It was a great relationship!

We hosted a few food drive parties. Instead of bringing a dish to pass or hor derves, we asked that they bring non perishable foods. I was happy that I had bought a house with a two car garage because we were yet again, exploding to a whole new level, turning my garage into it's own food pantry.

I began posting pictures on Facebook which put me on a first name basis with both my Fed EX and UPS delivery drivers. Packages were being delivered several times a week with everything from soup to nuts! Chewy was delivering pet supplies and food. Water, knapsacks, hand-warmers, socks, and clothes were arriving. Neighborhood friends from the Beacon Woods Club House and my gym also jumped on the bandwagon with donations. Church members wove matts out of plastic bags. I handed those out for use under sleeping bags which kept their sleeping bags dry. The plastic was easy to dry in the sun if it got wet. Generosity never went unacknowledged. Thank you notes were always hand written. On the occasions where donations were made anonymously, I took pictures of the items donated and sent a thank you across the internet.

# 7. United Association of Plumbers and Pipefitters

Continuing to trade pins on Facebook gave me a great deal of exposure. A brother I was trading with reached out to the U.A. Journal, a monthly magazine that all U.A. members receive. After sharing what my organization was doing, a journalist from the magazine called me to ask for an interview so that she could write a story. I was blown away when the story made the inside cover of the November 2018 issue.

### The Heart of the U.A.

*One local retiree making a difference with a pin.*

*"When plumbers and pipefitters local 777 state of Connecticut retire Paul Venti was working with tools as a plumber, he was very involved with the local community. Two years ago, he moved to Hudson, Florida and while driving passed the tent cities that were cropping up all over Florida, he came to a decision that he had to do something to help. He started purchasing and collecting non-perishable food and personal hygiene products for the homeless in his community. It wasn't long before the 67-year-old Venti was operating out of a well-organized food pantry in his garage. Three days a week with individual lunch bags in tow, he drives to various tent cities in Pinellas County. He's on a first name basis with many of the tenants and is welcomed at all of the camps. 'I give them peanut butter and jelly sandwiches, canned ravioli, pudding snacks, bottled water, oranges, and apples. I also went to the Dollar Store to buy, socks, underwear, wipes, bug spray, toothpaste, tooth brushes and toilet paper. I go to a camp just three miles from home and feed thirty-five peo-*

*ple. The need is overwhelming.' Brother Venti was financing this endeavor on his own and he admits he was going broke. He is an avid U.A. pin and sticker collector and has an impressive collection that he proudly displays in his living room wall. He is also a follower of the popular U.A. pin and sticker trades on Facebook. In order to help Finance his Good Deeds he was selling his entire prize pin collection. One of his U.A. brothers suggested he create a pin to sell with the proceeds entirely earmarked for the cause. He was sent $3,000 to get started. He had 900 pins and 1000 stickers created. Other U.A. locals have joined to help fight fund the cause. Brother venti pins States the U.A. family fighting the good fight on Hunger. All the proceeds from the sale of the pins continue to go toward food and supplies for homeless people in Hudson, Florida. Brother Venti's dedication was highlighted on a local TV station that was program called The Best of Tampa. He spends roughly $800 a month on his project. In two years, he has feed more than a thousand people. U.A members send him dog food thru a popular pet food website to assist the homeless with caring for their pets. Brother Venti said, 'You know they love their dog. Their dogs eat before they eat themselves.' He does more than just hand out food though. Brother Venti sits down and talks to the folks he's assisting. 'What I try to do is listen to their stories. I try to give them hope. I look into their eyes. I'll bring pizza and we just sit down and talk. It's the right thing to do. It breaks my heart to see a little kid come* *out of the woods with their mother.' Venti said it can become overwhelming but he perseveres. He said he narrows it down and works on a few folks at a time. 'I don't just want to put a Band-Aid on things. I don't want to just depend on me but they need a leg up. They have to take a step after they get the leg up.' Brother Venti is humble and quick to point out that it has been the UA Brotherhood and Sisterhood that has made this venture possible. 'I'm just a person in the kitchen stirring a pot.' It's only been a month since he started selling the stickers and pins and he's already overwhelmed with gratitude. 'There are 35 million Americans Who Gon go hungry every night and 17 million our kids.' He never judges and added that we haven't walked in their shoes. We don't know their individual situations. 'I'm just scratching the surface here. But I'll never stop what I'm doing. It's got to be done.' Brother Venti is onto something here. One man who cares can inspire an entire Village. And that's exactly what he's done. If you'd like to buy a pin with a sticker and help brother Venti Feed the Homeless in Pinellas County email him paulventi@ sbcglobal.net.*

# 8. Karen and Chevy

The first homeless person I met was a pretty 21-year-old young lady named Chevy. She was on the street corner three miles from my housing complex. I asked her if she was hungry. She replied yes so, I told her I would take her to Subway for lunch. Along the way we picked up her mom, Karen. Over lunch they started to share their story with me. Karen a recovering drug addict had a bad marriage. She told me how her husband beat her and Chevy so they left. They took refuge with a relative for a short while but with Karen still fighting her own demons, she and her daughter soon ended up on the street. Their street housing consisted of a small tent in back of a Wendy's behind the dumpster on Route 19. Not long after, I stopped to visit them bringing hot coffee and breakfast sandwiches. It has rained the night before soaking the only clothes that they had. We headed over to the laundromat. It gave them a chance to get inside for a while. When we returned to their "camp site" we discovered that someone had stolen their tent and sleeping bags. I reassured them and told them it would be alright. I told them not to cry. We went shopping for new tents, sleeping bags and some food items. Then I drove them to a new patch of woods about 10 miles south of Hudson, Florida. Together we set up their new camp. Karen, at the time was 49 years old with no teeth, Hep C and walking with a cane because of a bad hip. Chevy had never been to a prom never been on a date, to the movies or to dinner. She had never been to a school dance. I lost track of them for almost 4 months. When they did resurface, Chevy had to shave her head because of lice. Karen was looking very tired and run down. They told me they had relocated to a different County in Florida trying to make a better life for themselves. Unfortunately, it didn't work out which is what brought them back to the streets of Hudson. When I left Hudson, Florida in July of 2020 there were still there.

# 9. Lisa Pizza

I took a very special liking to a woman named Lisa. I gave her the name Lisa Pizza simply because she loves pizza. The aroma of pizza cooking at a pizza place near her camp used to make her hungry. The first time we met she was in the dumpster in back of a Big Lot store. She had found candy that had been thrown out because it was outdated which she offered to share with me. Lisa had gotten a lot of items from that dumpster including most of her food as I found out later when she invited me to her camp. Lisa was actually a homeless hoarder, afraid to let anything go because she was in such need. She had made a camp in the woods, a place she rarely came out from. The judgement of an unkind world led her there by folks telling her that she smelled and that she should get a job. So, she stayed in the woods a lot by herself decorating her camp coming out only to find supplies. Whenever we agreed to meet, I would blow my car horn signaling that I had arrived. Lisa would emerge from the woods welcoming me with a hug and a big smile.

Lisa was doing well when she worked as a commercial fisherman. She'd be out to sea for days at a time sometimes long lining and sometimes fishing for cod, pollock, tuna and swordfish. The bigger the catch the more money she would make. But it was very hard life with long hours and very little sleep. Eventually, arthritis in her hands disabled her, She could no longer fish. Out of work bills kept piling up. With her rent overdue she faced eviction. So, her life living in the woods behind a Big Lots Department store began. Showers were a rare luxury. When it rained, Lisa stands under a downspout with a bar of soap. I offered her a hotel room so she could take a hot shower and sleep in a clean bed. But she said she could not leave her camp because her whole life was there. Lisa knew if she left for even a short while, everything she had would be gone when she returned.

Lisa frequently asked me for socks and bug spray. There was always a problem with raccoons and rats stealing the little food she kept at her camp. Still, every time we visited, Lisa greeted me with a hug and

a smile. One afternoon, I got wind that Lisa had a
birthday coming up. I told some other homeless folks
to please get the word out that we were going to have
a pizza party for her birthday. I also stopped by the
Napa auto store new her camp to ask the manager if
we could have a little get-together with some homeless folks in his parking lot. He agreed and simply
asked that we clean up afterward. Come to find
out, the manager of the Napa auto store was once
homeless. My better half and I get an assortment of
pizzas, Buffalo wings, a dozen bottles of soda and a
huge birthday cake with Lisa's name on it wishing
her a happy birthday. We set up folding tables in the
parking lot. We had nearly 45 homeless folks share
in the celebration. We all sang happy birthday and
some of the homeless folks even gave her gifts mostly,
things they had made. It was quite the bash. I'll never
forget that day. Lisa felt like she belonged, that she
mattered. It was an awesome feeling for me and my
better half as well. That was truly a highlight of working with homeless. I still have the thank you note she
wrote.

A few days later, I went to check up on Lisa with
a bag of food. I blew my horn for her to come out
of the woods. When she emerged, I could tell by the
look on her face that something was wrong. She told

me the police had been there earlier in the day and told her she had till tomorrow to break camp, pack up all her stuff and get out of the woods or she would be arrested and taken to jail for trespassing. She started crying. "Paul, I have nowhere to go. I don't know what I'm going to do. Everything I have is in this camp." The next day I went to Lisa's camp. A construction crew was bulldozing the patch of woods where she had been living. Lisa was nowhere to be found. I have never seen her again. I miss her. She is always in my prayers.

# 10. Jimmy: An Army Veteran

On any given day we lose 22 veterans to suicide, often PTSD that has gone untreated or has spun out of control. My good friend Jimmy was one of them. He was a paratrooper with the United States Army for four years. After being discharged, he relocated to Hudson, Florida. The cold winters in his home town of Brockton, Massachusetts were getting the best of him. When we first met Jimmy had a big bandage on his arm and he was wearing a hospital wristband. I asked him if he wanted something to eat. Sitting on a small patch of grass we immediately became friends. We broke bread and talked for a long while and shared a prayer. He told me he was homeless because there was no room at the inn. Jimmy was on a two-year waiting list for veteran housing. The thought of our veterans having to wait for two years for housing is something I still can't wrap my head around. Jimmy was trying to cope with PTSD by drinking which over time, developed into cirrhosis of the liver. He finally confessed that the bandage on his arm was self-inflicted. He had cut himself with a broken piece of glass in order to go to the ER to get out of the weather and get something to eat. Of course, when he was released, the few pieces of clothing that he possessed and his sleeping bag were gone. I put Jimmy up in hotel for a week. He was so grateful. He couldn't wait to sleep in a bed with clean sheets. Jimmy sounded like an excited kid when he realized he would be able to use the hotel swimming pool.

I made it a point to visit Jimmy on every food run. We always said a prayer and he never asked me for anything. He was in proud of that. I told Jimmy that I would be out of town for a bit. I was headed to Connecticut to host the Kleen Energy memorial service. When I returned, I looked for Jimmy like I always did. But he was gone. He had walked out in front of a tractor-trailer truck doing 60 miles an hour on Route 19. The sad news shattered my heart. I really thought we could get him back on track with help. He used to tell me, "Paul, you're doing God's work." Jimmy is no longer fighting demons. May he rest in peace.

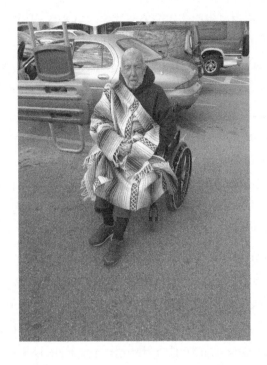

# 11. Eric, a 10 Year Veteran

The first week of every month you will not find Eric sitting in his wheelchair in the parking lot of Planet Fitness Gym. He's in a hotel room for that one week. That's all he could afford with his monthly check. I don't know if it's a social security check or veterans check, either way, that's all he can afford. You never told me and I never asked. But any other day of the month you can find Eric sitting in his wheelchair wrapped in a blanket. Usually he is under the overhang of a store front, a bit of protection from rain or the baking heat of the sun.

Eric served 10 years in the United States Army doing most of his time in Stuttgart, West Germany. Eric did not always play well with others and ended up with a bad conduct discharge. He is now 73 years old. He has made efforts to get help from the veteran's administration but he has difficulty with authority. He is head strong. Sometimes it is difficult to get the homeless back into the mainstream. Even my suggestion for us to visit the veteran's administration together was met with a definite no. Eric is known in the area that he hangs out in, the parking lot of the Winne Dixie. Folks will occasionally give him a few bucks and stop and talk. Some will give him hot meals.

Eric often wheels himself down to the library to escape the heat. He spends a good part of his day reading books and watching movies and tapes. When the library closes, he wheels himself back to the parking lot for the night. Definitely not the best quality of life. Although Eric is headstrong and stubborn, he deserves much better having served his country for 10 years. When I left Florida in July 2020 Eric was still sitting in his wheelchair in that parking lot.

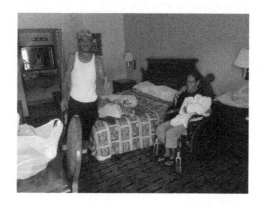

# 12. Husband and Wife

On one of my usual food runs, I came across a married couple named Margie and Dave. Margie was blind and was fighting lung cancer. Dave was a veteran who served in Afghanistan. He was working as a Furniture mover after being discharged from the service. Paid under the table in order to make ends meet, he never paid into social security or paid income taxes, something to this day, he regrets. Injuries to his back put him on disability permanently. He could no longer work moving furniture. The bills kept piling up. No unemployment insurance. He was however, receiving help from the veterans with his medical bills. Hoping to get back to work, he opted for back surgery. But it made little difference in his ability to do physical labor. That part of his life was over. On a two-year waiting list for housing with the VA, Dave and his wife Margie were evicted from their trailer for non-payment of their rent. But there is no rent to be paid living on the street, which is where they ended up. Margie was confined to a wheelchair as her respiratory conditioned worsened. They were both malnourished so the first order of business was to get them into a hotel and provide them with food. Being tourist season in Florida even the cheapest hotels were expensive. Funds were going out faster than they were coming in. But I made myself a promise that Margie would not die on the street. So, I did something I really didn't want to do. I raffled off my prize U.A. pin collection. I had loved collecting and trading them or just giving them as gifts to brothers and sisters just starting their collections or perhaps looking for a particular pin. But it really was a no-brainer. Let Margie die on the street or sell the pins. The sale of my pin collection helped get Margie and Dave a hotel room for weeks along with hot meals. A short time afterward, Margie headed into a sharp decline. We called an ambulance to the hotel and she was rushed to the hospital where she was admitted. Diagnosed with stage 4 lung cancer, Margie was moved to hospice. When I left Florida, Dave was still homeless awaiting housing for veterans.

# Photos

Carboard for his matress and napsack for his pillow

Dave Homeless Army Vet - why?

Didn't disturb his sleep but left him a breakfast beverage.

Homeless veteran looking to see what he can find for his camp, including outdated food that was thrown out.

Hudson cops making homless break camp or go to jail

Larry and his dog Hatch. You can tell Hatch eats better then he does.

Mattress made out of cardboard.

Old Rostabout. No matter how cold it gets outside he will not seek a shelter.

A single dad who wants to work but has to take his
children with him.

That is where one of our Vietnam homeless vets was
laying down to sleep

Your donations gave their kids a Christmas meal and Christmas presents and helped pay the rent.

# 13. A Man and His Dog.

Many of our homeless have dogs. They're their best friends and the homeless always put their dog before themselves. Pete's dog is named Bo. When you're homeless, your dog is your friend, your comfort, your security, your family. In short, your dog is everything. That was the case with Pete and Bo. Bo never leaves Pete's side. He is his shadow. Pete spends his days sitting on a concrete sidewalk in front of a convenience store making crosses and flowers out of Palms. He picks Palms from trees and sells them for a dollar each to feed his dog and himself. Pete sometimes has a hard time putting a sentence together. He sometimes talks in riddles. He has been in the street for three years but has never shared with me how he became homeless. There are many whose stories remain untold. But the obvious love of a man and his dog is real whether living in the finest home or living on the street.

# 14. Mother and Child

I only met this 5-year-old boy once. It was a Saturday morning near one of the camps that I used to visit. Being Saturday morning, was thinking this 5-year-old boy should be sitting down in front of the television with a bowl of Captain Crunch watching cartoons. Instead he was coming out of the woods where he spent the night with his mother. It was not a camping trip. It was where they lived. He gave me a high-five and a hug when I gave him a peanut butter and jelly sandwich and some fruit. His smile is hard to forget. I came back several more times but the little

boy and his mother had vanished. I asked a few of
the homeless about them. All I was told was that they
had moved. But no-one knew where that moved too.
I pray they are okay.

# 15. Another Life Lesson

The stories of our homeless are endless. I couldn't possibly share all of the stories of those I have crossed path with. But what I learned along the way has been priceless. Almost every homeless person I came in contact with always wore a smile. Most asked if we could share a prayer. Sometimes when there were only two or three bags of food left and I came across a group of five or six folks they were happy to share. Often, one would tell another, "I already ate today. You take it." Or, "I have some food back in my camp you can have this." There was never greed or selfishness. They helped one another. There was the occasional fight over turf. "This is My corner to pan-handle." I did notice some drug and alcohol use. But I don't work for the judgement business. Some, like Lisa Pizza, Dave, Margie, Chevy and her Mom were clean, sober. So many get used to life on the street. They grow accustomed to that lifestyle. Sadly, the longer they're on the stree,t the less likely they are to reintegrate into society. They're tired of people looking down at them, telling them to get a job or telling them they need to bathe. Eventually, they accept homelessness as their permanent station in life. But every homeless person is somebody's mother, father, sister, brother, husband or wife. They're human beings. Nobody is exempt from being homeless

# 16. Reasons People Become Homeless

People become homeless for a variety of reasons. However, the most common reasons are an inability to pay rent 63%; conflict or abuse 36%; alcohol or drug use 10%. Other factors include mental disorders, foster care or difficulty with the law. Homeless rates went up 17% in 2019 in California. This was mainly due to the high cost of living and the devastating wild forest fires. Folks could not bounce back after losing their homes. Some didn't have homeowner's insurance. Some are still fighting with their insurance companies.

# 17. CT. M.O.M.
# Bob Scheibman

It's funny how you cross paths with certain people in your life and why certain people stay in your life. One day I saw a gentleman on the elliptical at the gym and he was sporting a Connecticut Missions of Mercy t-shirt. I told him that I had seen his interview on the Channel 3 news about his upcoming work at the Hartford Civic Center. With that introduction and a handshake, we began a great friendship. Bob is the president of *Dental Outreach* and the Foundation of the Connecticut Missions of Mercy free dental care. One of the first health problems that the homeless encounter is with their teeth. Eating from dumpsters, eating foods with a high sugar content along with not brushing or seeing a dentist causes rapid tooth decay

and gum disease. Tooth decay and gum disease also
effect the body long term. The bacteria you're digesting
puts you at risk for heart disease, respiratory infec-
tions, and complications from diabetes. Bob Scheib-
man, Josephine De Lucia Bicknell, and so many other
volunteers work to combat these issues for those who
either do not have dental insurance or have no way to
pay for dental care. He told me to check out M.O.M.
website and I could volunteer. I was very impressed
when I went to the Hartford Civic Center in down-
town Hartford. M.O.M. had a tractor-trailer truck
come in with a hundred dental chairs. On the first day,
which happened to be a Thursday, we hooked up water
lines and suction lines to the dental chairs with the
help of a few apprentices and other members of local
777 plumbers and pipefitters. Friday was the big day. I
arrived before dawn at 3 a.m. Folks had been waiting
all night, sleeping in sleeping bags or in lawn chairs or
just on concrete. The line went on for blocks. Some of
these folks have not seen a dentist in decades. But no-
one is ever turned away. Some would need more than
one visit. They were welcomed back the next day for
follow up procedures. Some patients even sign up to
volunteer. Going to the dentist may seem like a small
thing but it is amazing how it effects one's self-esteem.
A healthy mouth allows the homeless, or anyone else

for that matter, to talk, smile, and laugh without covering their mouths because they are embarrassed about tooth decay. They are also more willing to go out for a job interview. They feel as though they can face the world with a little less judgement. I was amazed how one kindness; free dental care could restore someone's whole outlook. The project is one that involves roughly 400 volunteers, from the dentists, to the hygienists, UCON dental students, x-ray technicians, lab technicians not to mention the volunteers who do the set up and breakdown and those who provide food. More than 1000 procedures were performed over that one weekend.

A few days later, I meant Bob back at the gym. He told me I would be getting a phone call but wouldn't tell me what it was about. I was in awe when I was asked by the person on the other end of the phone if I would consider being a board member. Now it's a win-win situation. Not only could I bring some new ideas to the table at the board meetings, but Bob and Josephine asked me if I would like to incorporate my food drive with the mission. Using the M.O.M. database, we are able to send out eblasts asking for donations of non-perishable food items for Fighting the Good Fight on Hunger. So, at our next event, water, and canned goods were being donated by the case.

We received so many donations that we had to load it all onto two pickup trucks and then store the food at Local 777 Training facility. By this time, I had learned to expect the unexpected. These free dental events serve so many. An elderly lady was walking with a cane, hunched over and dressed kind of raggedy. She had had a dental procedure, the gauze still in her mouth when she approached me. "I didn't realize you were having a food drive," she said. I reassured he that just the staff and the volunteers knew about it. "I would like to donate." Reaching in her purse she pulled out a little change pouch and took out a crumpled up $5 bill. I explained that she didn't need to donate but she insisted. "I want you to have this." I had actually been thinking of giving her a bag of groceries. Instead, I took the $5 bill. When she handed it to me she grasped my hand and looked in my eyes. She said, "You see young man, I know what it's like to be hungry. I know what it's like to go to bed on an empty stomach not knowing when you're going to eat again or where your next meal was coming from. I'm doing just a little bit better now and I want to give back."

# 18. Donna Fineran: Brian O'Connell Homeless Project

My basset hound Dudley loves to take walks. I loved walking him in my Beacon Woods neighborhood in Florida. We were on such a walk one afternoon when a pickup truck stopped and complimented Dudley. The woman driving the truck said she too has a basset hound named Herman Walter. Not having any dog parks close by, she suggested that

we have a doggie play date. I have a fenced-in back-
yard. The following day she and her husband came
over with Walter Herman in tow. Noticing my food
pantry in the garage, she started telling me a remark-
able story that she had read in her monthly Catholic
magazine about a woman named Donna Fineran.
She is from Waterbury, Connecticut and works with
the homeless. After a lovely visit and a wonderful
playdate for our dogs, she offered to drop off the
article. A couple days later she dropped the article off
at my house. The story was both heart breaking and
amazing. I knew I had to meet this lady. Donna had a
twin brother, Brian that was homeless. After working
in New York City and witnessing 9/11, Brian had
a severe case PTSD (Post Trauma Stress Disorder).
It was so bad he could not work. Brian lived with
Donna and their family for a while and seemed to
be doing better. But on the 10-year anniversary of
9/11, Bran's PTSD triggered when he heard the bells
ringing during the memorial service of the victims
of 9/11. He moved out of Donna's house and built a
little Camp by the Naugatuck River. His body was
found on October 20, 2016 by a priest. Brain had
frozen to death. he state medical examiner released
his body in January pending an investigation that
include a DNA analysis in order to make a positive

identification. Father Sullivan, the priest who found
Brian, invited Donna and her husband to mass. At
the pulpit the priest asked the parishioners if they
would attend the funeral of a homeless man. Virtually
every hand went up to. Nearly 350 people attended
her brother's funeral, someone they didn't even know.
A few weeks later I was in Connecticut. Donna and
I went on a food run together. She later became one
of the speakers at one of the seminars that I hosted,
*Awareness on Homelessness and Hunger*. Donna's corporation, in honor of her brother makes *Brian's Bags*,
snacks, toothpaste, toothbrushes, and bottled water
which then she hands out to the homeless. She also
donates sneakers, socks and other toiletry items that
the homeless are in constant need of. The work never
ends shining a constant light on the loving memory
of her brother Brian.

# 19. Twist of Fate:
# Joanna Biondolillo, Author
# of When I Was a Child

Tommy Larkum is a childhood friend of mine. He sings in a charity band called Crossroads. Crossroads is a charity band with the primary goal of helping the charities improve the lives of others. They have also helped my organization with two food drives. Tommy call me one day and said he had just got back from an art exposition in South Carolina where he met this really cool artist, and author of a book about the homeless. Her name was Joanna Biondolillo, the book, "When I Was a Child".

Tommy sent me a copy. He mentioned that he had a friend that lived in Florida who also does work with the homeless. So, the first thing I did was reach out to Joanna. We were preaching to the choir! We talked for quite a long time and automatically became friends. I knew right then and there that we would cross paths. It was destiny. Now this beautiful young lady that has no fear. She crisscrosses the United States and on our own dime. She befriends and interviews the homeless where ever she finds them and always asks, "When you were a child, what did you want to be when you grew up?" Not one said, "When I grow up I want to be homeless." She has interviewed the homeless in Las Vegas Nevada tunnels and walked alone among the homeless on Skid Row in L.A. She has visited tent cities and homeless camps all over the country including Seattle, Washington and Miami, Florida. She documented their stories and wrote what the homeless say they need to get back into society. Joanna's journey with the homeless began a while back. This is what she wrote in the Preface of her book:

*"The seed for this journey, understanding home-lessness, was planted on a cold February night*

*when I was in college. I had stopped off to get a
cup of coffee on my way to class. A homeless man
wanted to use the bathroom in the coffee shop. "It's
only for customers," he was told. "But I got to go
bad!" The man was asked to leave. I just watched.
I did not understand. As I came out of the coffee
shop, the man was relieving himself against the
building. I looked up at the revolving clock at the
bank in the adjacent lot. The clock read, 5:00 pm,
and underneath the time was the temperature, four
degrees."*

What I admire about her she doesn't just talk the
talk she also walks the walk. She calls politicians and
emails government officials in an effort to pursue
legislation that will correct a system that fails hundreds
of thousands of it's citizens. sensor system. To this day
Joanna is still crisscrossing the United States to check
up on and help many of the homeless friends she made
on her journey. She continues to call politicians to try
and make them open their eyes about this ongoing
homeless problem. She is a role model and shares fac-
tual truths and verifiable statistics about the homeless.
Joanna also explains how we can get a handle on and
fix homelessness. Something she, herself learned from
the homeless. I highly recommend you read, When I
Was a Child: A Blueprint for Solving Homelessness in
America. You can download it for free at: www.wheni-
wasachildexhibit.com

# 20. Steve Zinn and the Portable Shower Trailer

Steve's Zinn was a welder out of Local 72 plumbers and pipefitters, Atlanta, Georgia. It wasn't uncommon for Steve or any welder to work on staging several stories high. While on a job that required Steve to be welding 33 feet off the ground, temporary lighting went out. Left to find his way in the pitch-dark he fell that 33 ft. to the ground. Guard rails had been removed from the staging. Steve broke both his arms, legs broke, ribs and pelvis. He was laid up in the hospital for months. The pain he was enduring was excruciating. Pain killers got him through it but that too came at a big price. Steve now had a monkey on his back. He was strung out on the Class A narcotics. Released from the Hospital Steve started to self-medicate. He had worked up a tolerance to pain medicine. Steve started doing some crazy things to make money to support his drug habit. He became homeless because all the money he got was going for drugs. He was also getting arrested. Steve finally ended up getting 14 years in prison. While in prison Steve had a lot of time to give himself a good talking to. He made a promise to the big guy. He asked the Lord to help him to stay clean and sober when he was released and in return, he would help feed one homeless person a day. Steve thought about what it was like to be homeless. One of the things he missed the most while being homeless was a hot shower. He decided to do more than feed just one person a day. Steve designed a shower trailer.

Having mechanical ability skills because of his trade and schooling, Steve came up with a great design. He brought his idea of a shower trailer to the business manager of Local 72 Atlanta, Georgia. It's discussed on the union floor at a meeting in front of the executive board. It is voted on and the funds and labor are approved to build Steve's dream shower trailer for the homeless. The Joint Apprenticeship Training committee set up the labor and Steve oversaw the work every step of the way. The finishing touches are put on. The showers are now built and tested. But before Steve can get hot showers to the homeless, he has to get permits, a water meter and a backflow preventer and permission from the water company to use a fire hydrant. They have to hire security to be at each location when they set up and he needs a few dozen volunteers to disinfect each shower after every use. Volunteers also hand out soap, shampoo, towels and clean underwear. They set up tables and chairs in order to serve food to the homeless that is donated by local restaurants. And of course, there is cleanup.

Steve is often the first one on the scene when there is a hurricane or wild fire. He called me back in October 2020 to say that he was headed to Baton Rouge to help out with the victims of the Hurricane Laura. He lost cell service to his iPhone. Not being able to track the storm he drove right into it. The hurricane literally picked up his heavy-duty truck and trailer. When he landed the trailer snapped off its hinge and flew into Lake Charles. Although his truck suspension was damaged, he was able to limp back to Atlanta. Steve had to make good on a water meter and backflow preventer he had rented and not having insurance for his trailer didn't help matters. Everything that he had worked for was once again gone in the blink of an eye. But he did not throw in the towel.

He is currently working to get funds to rebuild a new shower trailer and still helping the homeless on a daily basis anyway he can. There's no holding Steve back.

# 21. Ronnie McLellan

The first time I saw a Ronnie, he was hosting a memorial on the North steps of the Capitol in Hartford, Connecticut. He was honoring those who went to work and never came home. I was very impressed with the ceremony. It was well organized and all the speakers were on point. Little did I know that I would soon be sitting with Ronnie on the Connecticut AFL-CIO Safety Committee working on safety issues for all workers. Ronnie had a 40-year career with the state of Connecticut. He had witnessed exposure to various and deadly toxins over the years including asbestos and toxic ash. He spent a great deal of his time working to limit hazards in the work place. His goal was always to provide a safe work environment realizing that the most important thing for his co-workers was to be able to come to work feeling confident about their personal safety.

In 2007, Ronnie was elected president of the SEIU Local 511. He and his members passed legislation making it a crime to injury or kill a worker in a work zone. These laws continue to protect highway workers and workers in both the public and private sector. Every April 28th, Ronnie hosts the workers memorial. Although I have a few years on Ronnie, he is like a mentor to me. He helped me to organize the Kleen Energy Memorial service and has also been one of our speakers. He truly works for others.

# 22. Kyle Zimmer

Kyle Zimmer is the health and safety director
With Local 478 operator engineers. It was
a great learning experience to sit with him on the
health and safety committee with the AFL CIO. And
he too is very instrumental with organize the Klean
energy Memorial services for the last 10 years. He is
one of my speakers and he also speaks at the workers Memorial every April 28th at the North steps of
the capitol. Kyle spends most of his time traveling
across the country to different union halls speaking
to the rank-and-file about the ongoing problem with

the opiate crisis and suicide problem in the Building Trades. He educates and provides help. He is happy to sit down and have a coffee with you one-on-one and help in any way he can .He uses his experience as a first responder to listen and advocate for change. Kyle is like a big brother to the building trades.I admire his leadership.And honored to call him a friend.

# 23. Chelsea Benard

"Snug as a Bug" may seem like something you would say when you tuck your child into bed at night, but for Chelsea Benard it is far more than that. She and her husband make weighted blankets to help America's Vets or anyone with suffering P.T.S.D., anxiety disorders, or autism. The company she founded is called, *Snug as a Bug*.

I invited her to our Awareness Seminar on Homelessness to speak back in April of 2019. She shared some amazing success stories about her blankets including a story about a veteran that was not able to sleep with his wife for over 10 years because his post trauma stress disorder was so severe. After using one of her weighted blankets, he has now been able to sleep next to his wife. Every step we take can make a difference in someone else's life.

# 24. Road Trip

I was living in Florida, Joanna in South Carolina. Between us, Steve was living in Georgia. I had been wanting to go to Georgia to acknowledge brother Robert Buchelle, Executive Board member of local 72 plumbers and pipefitters. He was responsible for submitting a letter to the membership on two occasions resulting in donations of a sizable amount for the homeless. So, I called Joanna and Steve and made a plan to meet at local 72 Union Hall just outside of Atlanta. I also wanted to get more of an education on the issues facing our homeless. Who better than to educate me then Joanna and Steve? I loaded up my truck with several cases of bottled water, a variety of non-perishable food items and toiletries. I met Joanna a few miles from the hall and we headed over to the parking lot. We were greeted by the business manager Stephen Robert. We headed inside the lobby exchanging a few stories.

Joanna had given him one of her books and posters to the business manager. He hung the poster on the wall. Our next stop was Steve's house several miles away. Steve showed us the shower trailer but his truck was in repairs at the time so we did not do a shower run, unfortunately. We returned to his garage taking about the homeless while making up food bags so we could make our first food run of the day. With all the bags put together we jump in the truck. Our first stop was a convenience store nearby. There we met an older, homeless gentleman with no front teeth. He looked kind of husky but it was probably because he had layers and layers of clothes on. His nick name was Roustabout. He asked if he could have a second bag of food for another homeless friend. He has never accepted any kind of shelter. He said he'd rather take his chances living in the woods, no matter how much the temperature dropped. He said he trusted the shelters even less than being on the street. Instead he searched through garbage cans all day long at various convenience stores and supermarkets searching for old scratch off lottery tickets that people have thrown out. He said you'd be surprised how many winning tickets are discarded. He said he has had a few nice scores but never told us how much.

Our next encounter was with a beautiful lady with the nickname, "green eyes." She was truly beautiful. She was living in an abandoned house with no heat or electricity. In the middle of the floor was a gas generator which she used to generate heat. She spent most of her time trying to help other homeless folks, grateful that she has a roof over her head. It was common to meet those in desperate situations and yet they were trying to help those around them.

We continued that food run at different locations and on street corners handing out all the bags of food we had made up meeting quite a few interesting folks along the way. All have a story to share.

Night was starting to fall so we decided to have some dinner then head back to Steve's house. We sat around his kitchen table and we talked for hours. Early the next morning we had a cup of coffee and made a pact to meet again. We still keep in touch. I only wish that we could have done a shower run.

# 25. Homeless Shelters

When you see a homeless person pushing a shopping cart, their whole life is in that cart. When you see a homeless person with their dog, that dog is their best friend and the love of their life. You can't bring that dog or that shopping cart into a homeless shelter. Homeless shelters are known for bed bugs, body lice, fights, drug abuse, alcohol abuse, lack of counseling and cleanliness. Living in a shelter also means living among people you don't know or may not trust perhaps, even fear. Almost all the homeless folks that I talked to about shelters tell me that they would rather take their chances living in the woods, under a bridge or in on an abandoned car.

# 26. Mental Illness

The Connecticut Alliance of Retired Americans asked me if I would go to a Medicare summit in Washington D.C. to represent them. When I was leaving the hotel, I saw a man talking to a concrete wall and I knew right away he was homeless. I ducked into a coffee shop and bought a hot cup of coffee and some pastry. I walked back over to the man who was still talking to the concrete wall. "Here. Have something to eat." He looked at me for a brief second with vacant eyes, then turned back to the wall to continue his conversation. I continued on to the Medicare Summit. After a long day, nearly 10 hours later, I was returning to the hotel when I noticed the same man still talking carrying on a conversation with the wall. I remember how sad it was too see. Pennsylvania Avenue, about two blocks away from the White

House, was home to a lot of homeless people sleeping in sleeping bags on top of steam grates trying to stay warm. A nearby park was also full of the homeless. Unfortunately, federal and state governments look to cut budgets on every turn. Mental health services are often limited if they exist at all. Schizophrenia, paranoia and depression are plentiful among the homeless. I've met so many homeless people that could not even put a sentence together.

# 27. The Numbers

Each January thousands of volunteers attempt to count our nations homeless, city by city, county, by county in the Point in Time Census. It is only an estimate. This annual report is issued to Congress in the fall every year. The PIT however, weas never issued to congress in the fall of 2020 not because of COVID-19, but because Ben Carson of Housing and Urban Development simply did not release the information. Our homeless counts having been rising out of control over the past several years.

In 2019 we counted 567,715 homeless Americans. 350,642 of them were staying in emergency shelters; 217,073 were living in the woods, under bridges, in tent cities or in cars. The count includes 37,085 homeless veterans. But again, these are just estimates. The census prohibits including those who have found temporary shelter if only for one night. The homeless who have been incarcerated for even minor violations, meaning that they will be back on the street in a week or a month are not counted. If a homeless person is in the ER the night the counts are done, they are not counted. And if a homeless person is fortunate enough to have a voucher for a hotel for a short time, they are not allowed to be counted. Then there are those who will not be counted. They have given up.

Currently, the states with the highest percentages of homeless are, California, New York, Florida, Washington State, Texas, Massachusetts, Oregon, Pennsylvania, Georgia, and Ohio.

# 28. Why Not?

I'm sure you have a jacket, sweater or other clothing that you probably haven't worn in a while. Why not help keep a homeless person warm?

Before we go to bed at night we can walk over to the thermostat and turn the heat up if we are cold or we can put a bag of pellets in our pellet stove to keep warm A homeless person doesn't have that option. It can be as simple as something I saw in Florida. People were taking their unneeded jackets and scarves and tying them to telephone poles with a sign saying "It's yours for the taking." Why not??

I bet you have cans of tuna fish, soups, vegetables, pork and beans you didn't even know you had. Why not donate them to the local food pantry or if you see a homeless person give it to them? Could you imagine if we all gave up a bagel and a latte for just one a week? We can feed families. Instead of ignoring the homeless person outside of the coffee shop, why not pay for his/her coffee? The person you help could be a VET. Welcoming home our VETS is great but not enough. So many are living on the streets. They put their lives on the line for us and are now face a two-year waiting list for housing. I will never forget how my brother Tommy was treated when he returned from Vietnam. It was not good.

# 29. F.Y.I.

I am very proud to be a union man. Some people are not painting the picture with a big enough brush when it comes to unions. They are under the false impression that we are overpaid and we don't work hard. That couldn't be any further from the truth. It's always been 8 hours of work for 8 hours pay. Unions were created to protect workers from unsafe working conditions, and overzealous contractors. We are skilled craftsmen and women working on construction sites that demand that there be safety codes and those codes must be enforced. We build the schools where your children are educated. We build the hospitals where you seek care. We build the powerhouses where you get your energy from, and the ball parks where you seek to make memories with your children. The list goes on. The United Association of Plumbers, Pipefitters, and Sprinkler fitters do some awesome charity events that often goes unnoticed. Local 440 Indianapolis Indiana has a program called fill the Foxhole every year they make up Christmas packages for our troops that are deployed overseas. Local 21 from Poughkeepsie, New York bagpipe players drove all the way down to Middletown, Connecticut from upstate New York to perform at the 10-year memorial service for our fallen Brothers at Klean Energy in Middletown Connecticut out of respect Local 777 CT. Retiree Club host a holiday food drive for the AFL-CIO food pantry to help fight hunger. Local 333 from Lansing Michigan has a Christmas party and gives a Christmas meal and presents to 30 orphans from St Vincent's orphanage. Who would other wise not have one. Local 524 Scranton Pennsylvania sponsors a golf tournament that benefits St Joseph's Hospital. Local 420 Philadelphia Pennsylvania host of Monte Carlo night for Make-A-Wish Foundation. Local 598 in Pasco Washington gives bikes to children at Christmas time. And let's not forget what local 370 Flint Michigan did for the lead

crisis problem they had 370 plumbers pipefitters and
service technicians came together and changed out
water filters and plumbing fixtures . They donated
trucks loaded of bottled water so people could have
Drinking water. And not for recognition but simply
because it was the right thing to do. And the list goes
on and on. That is Solidarity. And if that what being a
Union Thug is all about—then I am damm proud of
being a Union Thug.

# 30. Counting Our Blessings

Ask yourself, *how much more do I really need?* We are blessed to have a roof over our heads, a hot shower, a comfortable bed, food in the refrigerator. The homeless have taught me to be thankful for what I do have. I no longer think about what I don't have. When you wake, ask yourself what can I do to make someone's life just a little bit better that day. One simple act of kindness will also make your day a little better. Put a smile on someone's face. It will come back to you. Help us to fight the good fight on hunger and homelessness.

# About the Author

Paul Venti is the founder and president of Fighting The Good Fight On Hunger And Homelessness a nonprofit corporation that was founded in 2016. A former board member with people helping people fighting hunger. Volunteers and coordinates food drives with Missions of Of Mercy M.O.M. Free dental clinic. Hosted various awareness seminars regarding fighting hunger and homelessness has taken on the battle as a personal challenge in the hope to help lift fellow citizens out of there plights. Retired member of Plumbers and Pipefitters Local 777 in the state of Connecticut and was the food Drive Coordinator for his Local Union. As a Proud Union member held many leadership positions such as Executive Board, Chairman of the retirees Club, and Trustee on the health fund. And have been elected by his  peers to represent plumbers and pipefitters local 777 as delegate 3 times for the  U.A. General Convention. For the past 11 years hosted a memorial service For our Fallen brothers that were lost at the gas explosion in

Klean Energy Middletown Connecticut. February 7th 2010. Sat on the health and safety committee with the AFL-CIO for the workers Memorial. Represented the Connecticut Alliance for retired Americans twice in Washington DC for Medicare and Social Security. Received the Kevin Lynch award from The Connecticut Alliance for retired Americans. Received the Ed Egan Courage award for health and safety from CT. COSH. The Connecticut Council On Occupational Safety And Health. Received an official citation from representatives Matthew Lesser and Linda Orange for leadership and advocation on behalf of victims of the Klean Energy tragedy. The Michael Petosa Health and Safety award. For leadership and commitment for health and safety in the workplace.

Find me on YouTube:

Fighting the Good Fight on Hunger and Homelessness:
https://www.youtube.com/watch?v=GneJo9wA6Ig&t=121s
https://www.youtube.com/watch?v=Kzp269SBum0

Anyone wishing to help fight hunger can PayPal me at
**paulventi@sbcglobal.net**

*"To make a difference in someone's life you don't have to be brilliant Rich beautiful or perfect you just have to care."*

—Mandy Hale

*"Don't criticize what you don't understand."*

—Bob Dylan

Made in the USA
Monee, IL
21 April 2021